Prestel Publishing Ltd.
14-17 Wells Street
London W1T 3PD

Prestel Publishing
900 Broadway, Suite 603
New York, NY 10003

In respect to links in the book, the Publisher expressly notes that no illegal content was discernible on the linked sites at the time the links were created. The Publisher has no influence at all over the current and future design, content or authorship of the linked sites. For this reason the Publisher expressly disassociates itself from all content on linked sites that has been altered since the link was created and assumes no liability for such content.

Library of Congress Control Number: 2018965316
A CIP catalogue record for this book is available from
the British Library.

Translated from the German by Paul Kelly
Copyediting: Brad Finger
Project management: Melanie Schöni
Herstellung und Satz: Susanne Hermann
Druck und Bindung: DZS, Grafik
Papier: Tauro Offset

Verlagsgruppe Random House FSC® N001967
Printed in Slovenia

ISBN 978-3-7913-7403-1
www.prestel.com

Great Streets of the World

From LONDON to SAN FRANCISCO

Frauke Berchtig ◆ Agustí Sousa

PRESTEL

Munich ◆ London ◆ New York

Unter den Linden

BERLIN | GERMANY

In times gone by, the king of Prussia would ride west from his palace on Unter den Linden street to his royal hunting grounds. Berlin was just a small town in those days. Its zoo stood just outside the city walls. Today, Unter den Linden (which means "under the lindens") is the main thoroughfare of Germany's capital city, where over 4 million people live. Flocks of tourists stroll under more than one hundred linden trees that line the way towards the Brandenburg Gate and to the newly built palace.

Regent Street

LONDON | GREAT BRITAIN

This street really does go round the bend! At its middle section, it turns in a circular arch, and bus riders may feel like they're on a merry-go-round. Many buses travel on Regent Street, mostly the famous red double-deckers. Loads of pedestrians make their way to the nearby shops and department stores. Regent Street is named after a prince who went on to become King George IV. He served as "prince regent," or acting ruler, during the last years of his sickly father, George III. The road was completed in 1825.

La Rambla

BARCELONA | SPAIN

La Rambla is the most famous street in Spain. Everyone who visits Barcelona takes a stroll under its huge, 150-year-old sycamore trees. This grand promenade runs more than 1 kilometer (0.6 mile) in length, and it contains many different sections. Each section has a name, which sometimes refers to the goods being sold there—such as "flowers" or "crafts." Other names come from the local street performers or from nearby buildings. All of these different parts of La Rambla make it seem like more than one street, which is why people often call it by its plural name: "Las Ramblas."

Prinsengracht (Prince's Canal)

AMSTERDAM | NETHERLANDS

Amsterdam is close to the sea, so there is a lot of water in the city. Canals and other waterways flow along city streets. On the banks of Prince's Canal stand beautiful old buildings once owned by wealthy merchants. "Floating apartments," or houseboats, can also be seen. One of the narrowest old buildings is home to a museum called the Anne Frank House. Anne Frank was a Jewish girl who had hidden with her family in this house to escape the Nazis during World War II. In her world-famous diary, she wrote about this terrible time.

Chora of Mykonos

(The Old Town of Mykonos)

MYKONOS | GREECE

Mykonos is a Greek island in the Aegean Sea. The largest town, or "chora," on the island is called Mykonos, too. Gleaming white houses with their sky blue shutters stand extremely close to one another. The streets and alleyways are so narrow that, depending on the sun, one side is bathed in light while the other remains in shade. People in Mykonos like the shade, as it can get very hot in the summer. There is no room for cars on these winding streets. Only nimble little scooters can pass through.

Rue des Abbesses

PARIS | FRANCE

Oh là là—there is a luring fragrance in the air! Does it come from the freshly-baked croissants on the charming bistro tables, or from the flowers in the market stall? Montmartre is also a feast for the eyes, from the bright white church of Sacré Cœur to the elegant artworks that can be seen everywhere. Since the 19th century, this charming district in Paris has attracted painters from all over the world. Some of them became world famous, including Pablo Picasso and Vincent van Gogh. Today, artists place their easels right on the street, and tourists can even peer over their shoulders as they work. In the evenings, the view of Paris from Montmartre hill is breathtaking.

Rynok Square

LVIV | UKRAINE

Oops! This is not a street. It's the marketplace of Lviv in Ukraine, known as Rynok Square. A marketplace is usually at the center of town, where all the streets come together. That's why Rynok is in our book of streets. Lviv has a long history. The houses around the marketplace were built in many different time periods over the last 400 years. You can find different styles of architectural there, from renaissance to baroque to art nouveau.

Hatogaya

SHIRAKAWA | JAPAN

Come with us on a trip into history. The homes on this street in Shirakawa, Japan look much as they did hundreds of years ago. The sloping, thatched roofs prevent snow from piling up on top of the houses, which is important because a lot of snow falls in this remote mountain region during winter. Extended families live in Hatogaya's homes, spending most of their time on the lower level. Traditionally, they would use the attic for cultivating silkworms.

Grand Canal

VENICE | ITALY

This street may be the strangest one of all! And that's because it is not really a street, but a canal. The city of Venice is unique in the world. It was built on marshy ground in the middle of a lagoon. Venice's beautiful buildings are supported by millions of tree trunks—or "piles"—that are sunk deep into the ground. Magnificent palaces, churches and houses would collapse into the water without this wooden foundation. The 118 islands that make up Venice are connected by more than 400 bridges. Instead of cars or buses, boats take people from one part of the city to another. The most elegant of these boats, called gondolas, are very popular with tourists.

Lombard Street

SAN FRANCISCO | USA

Is this a road or a roller-coaster? Lombard Street zigzags over Russian Hill, one of the 42 hills in San Francisco, California. It was designed with numerous turns and bends because the hill is too steep for cars to go down in a straight line. The road passes through a green district containing many beautiful gardens. Next to the street, steps enable tourists to enjoy fantastic views across the city.

Calle 3

MEDELLÍN | COLOMBIA

The district of San Javier, where Calle 3 street is located, has witnessed something of a miracle. Ten years ago, its residents barely dared to go outside. There were constant clashes between the army and drug gangs. Today, however, residents and tourists alike feel safe to stroll through San Javier's pretty streets and well-maintained parks. A huge escalator can take you up effortlessly past colorful houses and into the loftier area of the district.

Rua da Bica

LISBON | PORTUGAL

There is no escalator in this street, but you can easily reach your destination with the "elevador," or funicular. A funicular looks like a streetcar, but it is powered by a rope pulley system.
Of course, you can always try walking the 41 meters (135 feet) to the top. The route, which passes by beautiful houses with magnificent front doors and lush green balconies, is definitely worthwhile. And don't forget to take a photo! Rua da Bica is among the most famous sights in Lisbon.

Hàng Bac

HANOI | VIETNAM

Hàng Bac means "the street of silver crafts." It is one of 36 streets in the old town of Hanoi, Vietnam that are named after the goods being sold there. Hanoi also has a "ladder" street, a "spice" street and a "shoe" street. In earlier days, you could locate "the street of silver crafts" by sound alone because of the hammering of the silversmiths. Nowadays, the loudest noises come from the rattle of mopeds. Whole families, including their pets, use these small vehicles to travel around the city.

Calleja de las Flores

CÓRDOBA | SPAIN

This picturesque alley is extremely narrow, and many of the balconies have little room for flower pots. That is why the residents simply hang flowers on their walls. Córdoba is a city in Andalusia, a region in southern Spain. It's warm most of the year there, and the residents of the town like to party. During many of these "fiestas," the houses and courtyards are richly decorated with flowers, just like the ones we see here in the Calleja de las Flores—the "Alleyway of Flowers."

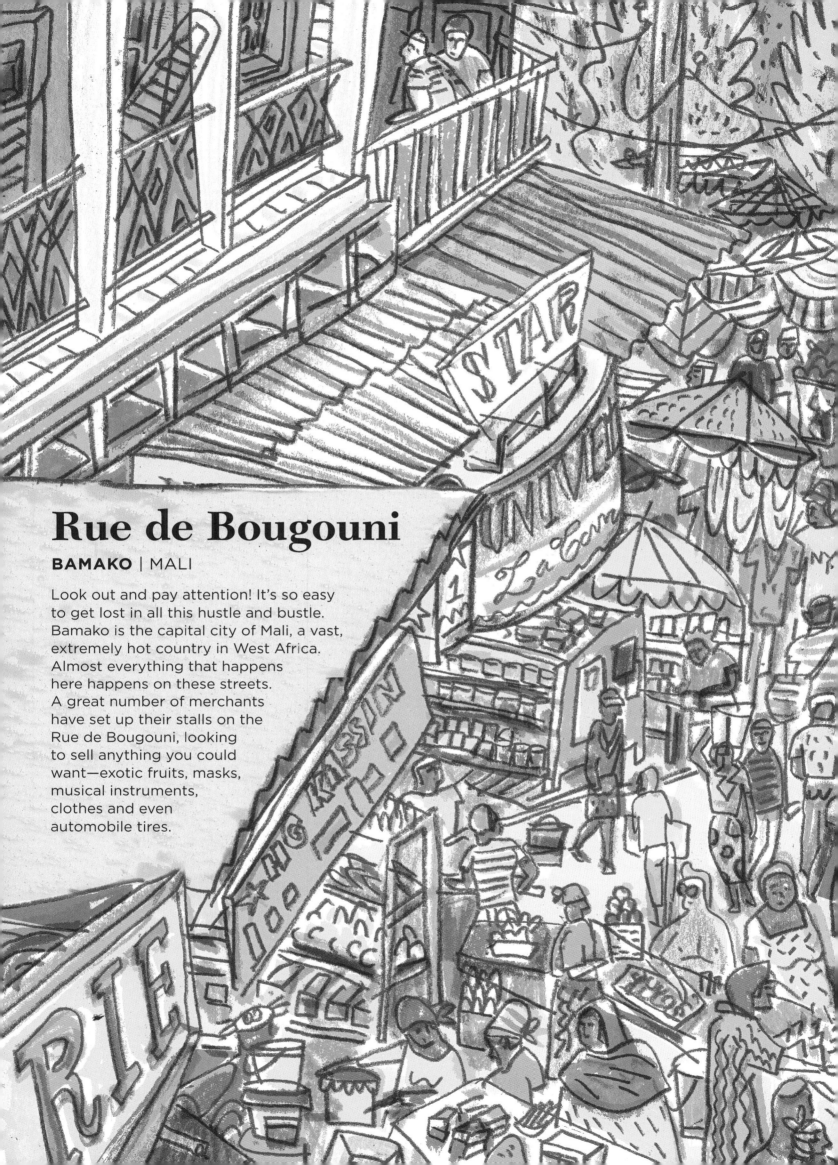

Rue de Bougouni

BAMAKO | MALI

Look out and pay attention! It's so easy to get lost in all this hustle and bustle. Bamako is the capital city of Mali, a vast, extremely hot country in West Africa. Almost everything that happens here happens on these streets. A great number of merchants have set up their stalls on the Rue de Bougouni, looking to sell anything you could want—exotic fruits, masks, musical instruments, clothes and even automobile tires.

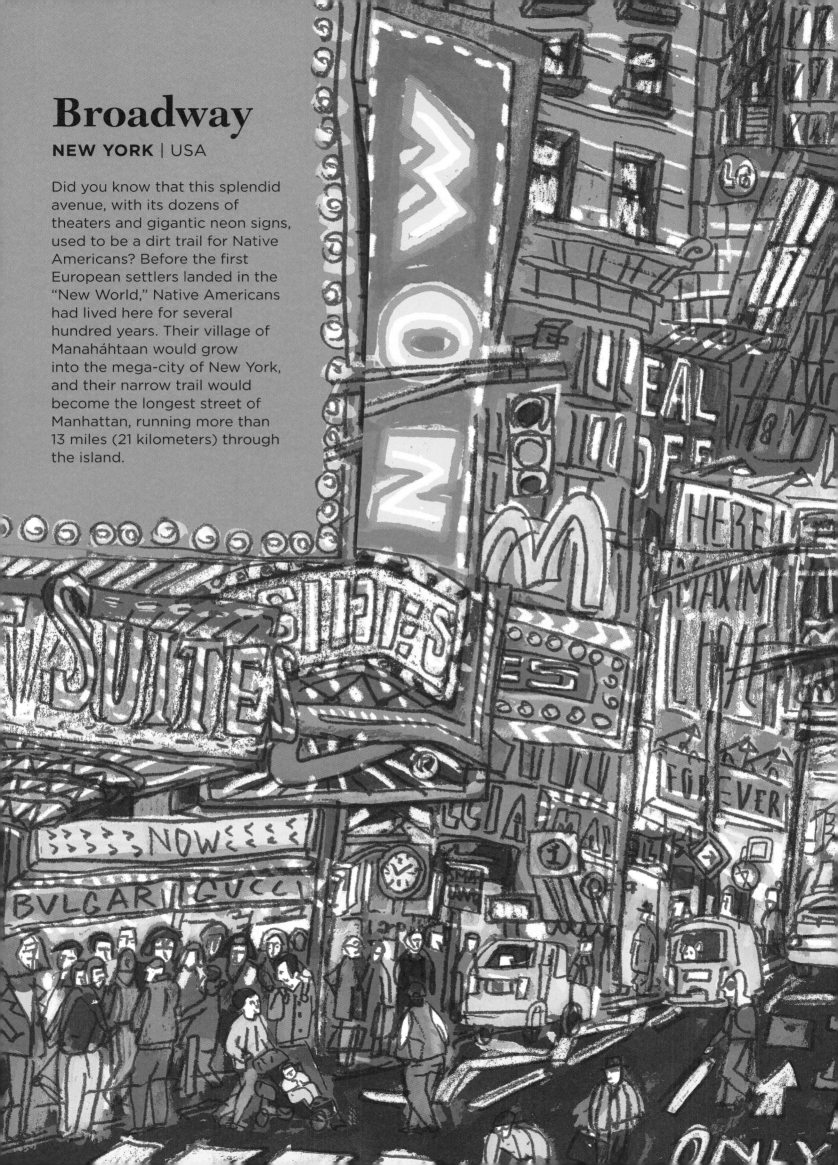

Broadway

NEW YORK | USA

Did you know that this splendid avenue, with its dozens of theaters and gigantic neon signs, used to be a dirt trail for Native Americans? Before the first European settlers landed in the "New World," Native Americans had lived here for several hundred years. Their village of Manaháhtaan would grow into the mega-city of New York, and their narrow trail would become the longest street of Manhattan, running more than 13 miles (21 kilometers) through the island.